DK Easy Peasy
CHINESE

走
中 文
向

Mandarin Chinese
for beginners

LONDON, NEW YORK, MUNICH,
MELBOURNE, AND DELHI

Written by Elinor Greenwood
Designed by Hedi Gutt, Gemma
Fletcher, Tory Gordon-Harris, and
Clare Shedden
Editor Carrie Love

Publishing Manager Susan Leonard
Art Director Rachael Foster
Production Claire Pearson
DTP Designer Ben Hung
Jacket Editor Mariza O'Keeffe

Consultants Katharine Carruthers
and Yu Bin

A CIP catalogue record for this book is
available from the British Library

ISBN 978-1-4053-1863-1

Colour reproduction by ICON,
United Kingdom
Printed and bound in China

Discover more at
www.dk.com

Contents

走 吧!

zǒu ba! **Let's go!**

Foreword

Five good reasons to learn Chinese:

1 China has the biggest population in the world – 1.3 billion people

2 If you speak English and Mandarin you can communicate with over half the world's population

Hi!

你好!
Nǐ hǎo!

3 China is becoming an economic superpower

4 The Chinese language is fascinating

5 You get much more out of a visit to China if you can speak some Chinese

That's great!

太好了!
Tài hǎo le!

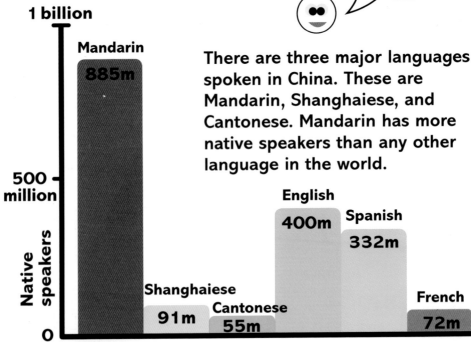

There are three major languages spoken in China. These are Mandarin, Shanghaiese, and Cantonese. Mandarin has more native speakers than any other language in the world.

1 billion

Native speakers

- **Mandarin** 885m
- 500 million
- **Shanghaiese** 91m
- **Cantonese** 55m
- **English** 400m
- **Spanish** 332m
- **French** 72m
- 0

中
Zhōng
文
wén

Mandarin has many different names in Chinese. Here are some, with their literal translations:

Guóyǔ	**national language**
Pǔtōnghuà	**universal words**
Hànyǔ	**language of the Han**
Zhōngwén	**Chinese language**

Chinese people learn Mandarin too

At the fall of the Qing Dynasty in 1911, the incoming nationalist government decided that Mandarin should become the standard language of China, replacing the many languages and dialects that made communication between people difficult.

It was originally thought that Mandarin would be spoken by everyone by 2030. However, because of the size of China and the number of languages spoken, teachers in many schools still give classes in the local language. Mandarin is studied like a foreign language class, to use for speaking with non-locals.

Using this book

You can take what you like from this book – an overview of the culture, with some insight into the language on the way, or use it as a study aid to become a competent beginner. Whatever your approach, this book is a good place to start.

The secret to learning Chinese is:

慢慢来！ Màn màn lái! **Take it easy!**

Pinyin

Pinyin is the name of the system we use to spell out the sounds of Chinese words in roman letters. It is a written aid to pronunciation.

No alphabet

Chinese writing doesn't use an alphabet. Instead it is made up of a series of **characters** each of which are made up of mini pictures. We need help to know how to pronounce them, and that's where pinyin comes in.

For example, how do you say this character?

Using pinyin, you pronounce it 'māo' (and it means 'cat').

Without knowing pinyin, it is very difficult for people to learn Chinese as a foreign language.

It is important to remember that pinyin is only a guide. The best way to learn the sounds of any language is to copy what you hear.

So put on the CD!

In this book, when you see this symbol, you can hear what is on the page by listening to the accompanying CD.

About pinyin

Pinyin was adopted by mainland China in 1958 and is the romanisation system used there today, and in this book. Other systems, such as 'Wade Giles', do exist though they are used less and less.

These are the characters for 'pinyin'

This means 'to spell'   This means 'sound'

How to use it

Chinese words are made up of one-syllable sounds, such as 'ma'.

❖ These sounds all start with an **'initial'**.
In the word **'ma'**, the initial is the **'m'** sound.

❖ And they all end with a vowel sound called a **'final'**.
In the word **'ma'**, the final is the **'a'** sound.

On the next few pages there are tables, first for the initials, then the finals. It is really worth going through each sound with the accompanying CD.

Table 1: Initials

Initial	Sound	Rough English sound
b	baw	bore
p	paw	pore
m	maw	more
f	faw	fall
d	duh	done
t	tuh	tore
n	nuh	nail
l	luh	late
g	guh	guard
k	kuh	come
h	huh	loch
j	gee	jeep
q	chee	cheese
x	she	ship
z	dzuh	'ds' in suds
c	tsuh	'ts' in cats
s	suh	see
zh	jir	germ
ch	chir	chin
sh	shir	shirt
r	rj	rank
w	ooh	swoon
y	ee	ye

This sound is between 'ship' and 'sip'.

Spread your lips in a smile and curl your tongue up so the tip touches the roof of your mouth.

Table 2: Finals

Final	Sound	Rough English sound
a	ah	**a**re
ai	i	**eye**
ao	ow	**ow**l
an	ahn	**an**t
ang	ahng	b**ang**
o	aw	str**aw**
ong	oong	**too + ng**
ou	oh	**g**o
e	uh	d**u**h
ei	ay	s**ay**
en	un	tak**en**
eng	ung	l**ung**
er	ar	**are**
i	ee / uh	**tea** / h**uh**
ia	ya	**ya**k
iao	yaow	m**eow**
ian	yan	**yen**
iang	yahng	**y + ang**st
ie	yeh	**ye**s
in	een	d**in**
ing	eeng	mow**ing**
iong	yoong	**you + ng**
iu	you	Cl**eo**

> 'i' is generally pronounced 'ee' except after these initials: c, ch, r, s, sh, z, zh when it is 'uh'.

Final	Sound	Rough English sound
u	oo	m**oo**
ua	wa	s**ua**ve
uo	waw	**war**
ui	way	**way**
uai	why	**why**
uan	won	**oo-won**
un	un	w**on**
uang	wahng	**wan + ng**
ü	yoo	**you**
ue	oo-weh	**you + eh**
üan	ywan	**you + wan**
ün	yewn	**you + n**

To make the ü sound, try saying 'ee', but through pursed lips.

Using the tables

When you see a word in pinyin:

1 Look up the first letter or two letters, which are usually consonants, on the **Initials table**.

2 Then look up the last letter or letters, which begin with a vowel, on the **Finals table**.

3 Put the two sounds together, and hey presto!

Practice time

track 3

Listen to the pronunciation of these words on the CD, then copy what you hear.

1. yi   **6.** qing   **11.** quan

2. zhong   **7.** xi   **12.** cong

3. cui   **8.** cai   **13.** zai

4. qiu   **9.** re   **14.** duo

5. yue   **10.** shi   **15.** nü

Pinyin pointers

- You need to look at each word carefully – they can look similar, but have very different meanings.

zǒu — to go

zuò — to sit

- Many words in Chinese are made up of more than one sound. You tell where each sound ends and each new sound begins by using the initials as markers.

xièxie **thank you**

↑ ↑

initials

↓ ↓ ↓

pǔtōnghuà **mandarin chinese**

- Pinyin also includes 'tone marks'. Turn over to find out what these are for...

🎧 The tones

Mandarin Chinese has four tones, and one 'toneless' tone. The tone you use when pronouncing each one-syllable word determines the meaning. The tone marks ¯ ´ ˇ ˋ show which tone to use.

1 1st tone – high level

Pitch your voice high and hold the sound there slightly longer than seems natural.

mā

mother

As a doctor tells you when looking down your throat. Say:

 Aaah!

2 2nd tone – rising

From the middle level of your voice range to the top. Raise your eyebrows as you say it!

má

hemp

The tone at the end of a question.

 What?

Tone deaf?

The tones may seem complicated, but you will soon get the hang of them. Consider these facts:

- There are more tonal languages in the world than non-tonal.
- Cantonese has at least 8 tones. Imagine that!

The 'neutral' tone

This isn't exactly a 'tone'. It is just a light way of saying a word. Pronounce it as you would say a word in English with no emphasis. It has no tone mark.

3 3rd tone –
falling and then rising

From the middle level, down deep, then up a bit.

mă

horse

Like when you're surprised.

Really?

4 4th tone –
falling

A short, sharp fall from your high voice pitch. Stamp your foot as you say it!

mà

scold

The tone of a statement.

No!

- China has over 80 dialects, and for many Chinese people, Mandarin is not their first language – Chinese people can make mistakes with their tones, too.

- People who can't sing a note (or are 'tone deaf') may feel they can't learn Chinese, but this is not the case. It makes no difference as tonal languages are relatively pitched, not absolutely pitched.

🎧 Learning the tones

If you don't learn the tones, quite simply, people will find it hard to understand what you say. Practise your tones by saying these words and listening to them on the CD.

1 māo
cat

6 shù
tree

2 yuè
moon

7 chē
car

3 gǒu
dog

8 yáng
sheep

4 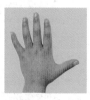 rén
person

9 shū
book

5 shǒu
hand

10 máo
feather

ying tones in a row

e you have grasped saying single-sound words
tones, try to put a few together, as you will need
so when speaking Chinese.

sháozi
spoon

This syllable is
the neutral tone.

dìtú
map

xióngmāo
panda

Don't worry
about making
funny faces while
you try to get
the tones right.

gōnggòngqìchē
bus

xīnnián kuài lè!
happy new year!

BANG!

Characters

The Chinese writing system is one of the most beautiful and ancient writing systems in the world. Before you start getting to grips with it, it's worth taking a few minutes to find out a bit about it.

Two styles

There are two forms of writing in existence today. The 'traditional' characters are still used in most Chinese-speaking countries outside mainland China. Mainland China predominantly uses 'simplified' characters and the simplified characters will be used in this book.

cloud – simplified

cloud – traditional

How many characters are there?

Altogether? More than **40,000** – though many are very rare. **2,000** characters are needed for basic literacy (or to read a Chinese newspaper).
A well-educated person in China would know **4,000–5,000**.

Top to bottom...

... right to left. Traditionally Chinese characters have been laid out in the opposite way to English (though most modern publications follow the Western way).

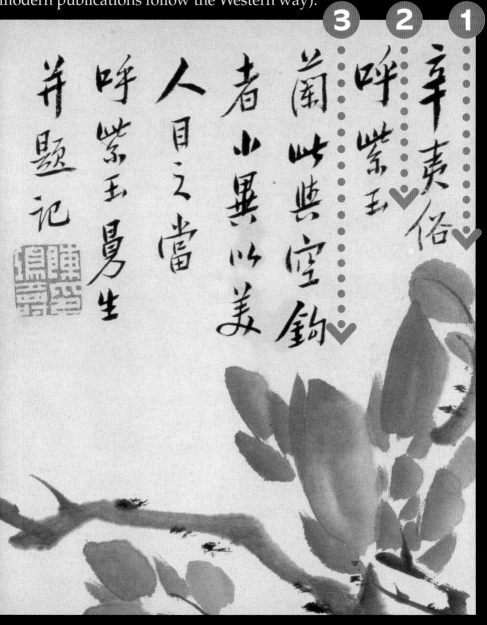

Start reading here.

3   **2**   **1**

Four types

There are four different types of Chinese characters that you will learn to write. These intermingle with each other in any block of Chinese text.

tree

Pictographs

The character is a picture of something. For example the character for 'tree' looks like a tree.

one

Ideographs

The character is a picture of an idea. For example the character for 'one' is just one line.

'One' on a die is also an ideograph.

Putting them together

The Chinese expanded their written language by putting pictographs or ideographs together to make new characters.

good

This is a pictograph for 'woman'.

This is a pictograph for 'child'.

女 + 子 = 好

woman **child** **good**

Ancient Chinese people thought 'woman' and 'child' together was 'good'.

---

yuǎn
far

yuán
garden

Phonographs

To expand the language further, the meaning of one character was combined with the sound of another to make phonographs. For example, the characters for 'far' and 'garden' share the same part that gives them their pronunciation: 元 (yuán). Their meanings are given by the other parts of the characters.

sound   meaning   a new character

元 + 辶 = 远   **far**
                              yuǎn
yuán   **to walk quickly**

元 + 口 = 园   **garden**
                              yuán
yuán   **enclosure**

Note: the sounds of the characters are almost the same – but they have different tones.

Different strokes

The writing of Chinese characters follows strict rules. The first thing to understand is that characters are made up of set strokes. These strokes are always written in the same way. Here are some basic strokes you need to write beautiful characters.

Follow the arrows that show the direction of the strokes, and practise copying them.

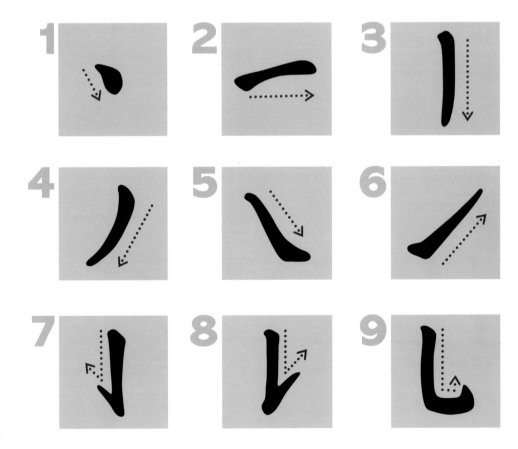

These are what brush strokes look like. Yours will probably look thinner.

Trace this table to practise.

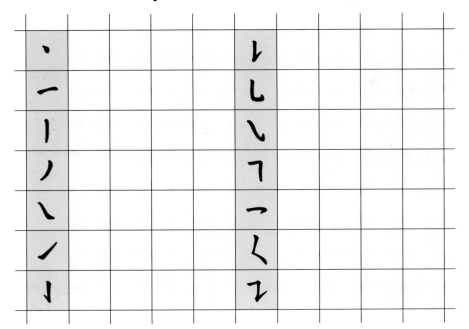

Stroke order

The order in which you write the strokes is also important. For one thing, getting the stroke order right makes the characters easier to learn. The two general rules to follow are:

1 Write **top** to **bottom**

2 Write **left** to **right**

Practise writing this character:

huà

word

Start with the part of the character that is on the top left.

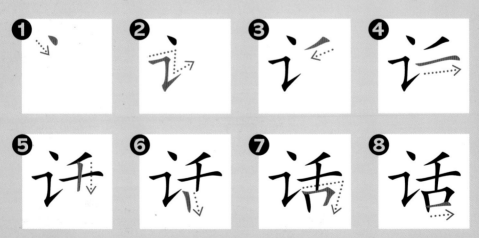

These rules are not fail-safe, however, as some characters are written with differing stroke orders.

  shí **ten**

left to right,
then top to bottom

    yuè **month**

first outside,
then inside

 xiǎo **small**

the middle,
then two sides

It all depended on what looked best or which order minimised blobbing when scholars were using brushes and ink to write.

How characters are made

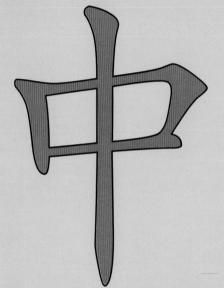

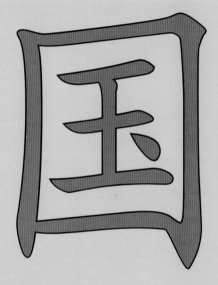

zhōng

中 means 'middle'

guó

国 means 'kingdom'

The **Middle Kingdom**

is what we now call

China

Be square

When you write each character, imagine you are writing it inside a square. You can buy or make squared paper for this purpose. Your characters will look more beautiful if they are evenly spaced, fit into equal-sized squares, and look symmetrical.

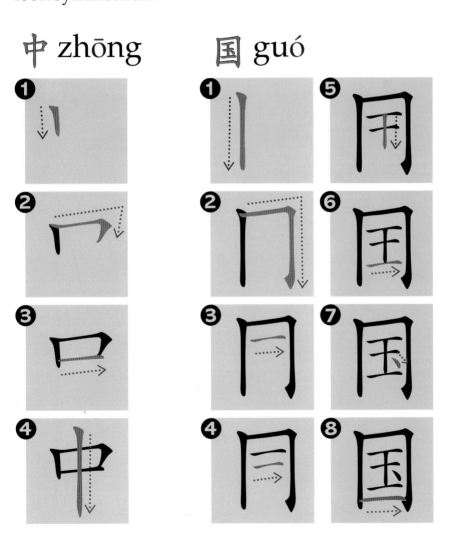

中 zhōng   国 guó

Memory tips

There is no really easy way to learn characters. Each one needs to be memorised. However, here are some pointers to help you.

- If you try to imagine a character as a picture, or if you know the origins of a character (see opposite for some examples), it makes it easier to remember.

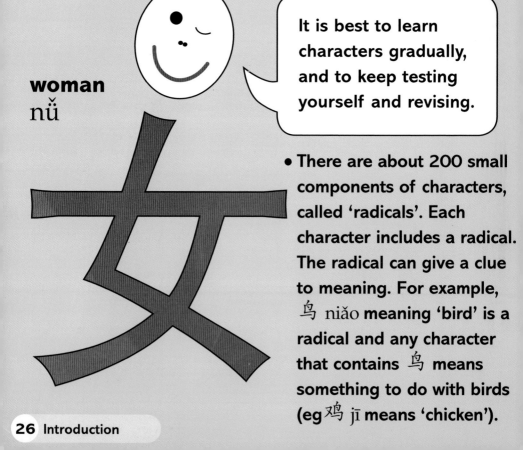

woman
nǚ

It is best to learn characters gradually, and to keep testing yourself and revising.

- There are about 200 small components of characters, called 'radicals'. Each character includes a radical. The radical can give a clue to meaning. For example, 鸟 niǎo meaning 'bird' is a radical and any character that contains 鸟 means something to do with birds (eg 鸡 jī means 'chicken').

Picture it!

Characters that are pictographs often look like the original pictures that were drawn centuries ago.

rì **sun**

yuè **moon**

shān **mountain**

shuǐ **water**

niǎo **bird**

mǎ **horse**

It's radical

Practise writing these characters. They are useful ones to know as they can also be found in other characters as 'radicals'.

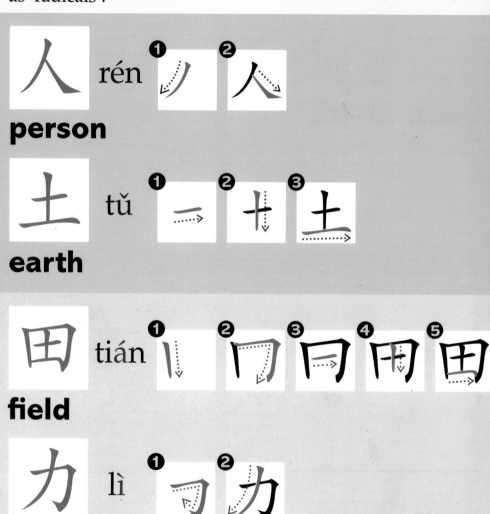

人 rén

person

土 tǔ

earth

田 tián

field

力 lì

strength

Put the characters together...

... to make new characters. Notice how the meanings of the new characters are directly related to the meanings of the original characters. It made sense in Ancient China.

坐 zuò

to sit

① 丿　② 人　③ 人丿　④ 人人

⑤ 𠈌　⑥ 坐　⑦ 坐

人 + 人 + 土 = 坐

Literally: people [on top of] earth

男 nán

man

① 丶　② 冂　③ 日　④ 田

⑤ 田　⑥ 毘　⑦ 男

田 + 力 = 男

Literally: strength [in a] field

Easy peasy
grammar

track 6

'Easy peasy' and 'grammar' don't usually go together, but here's an area of Chinese where there is less to learn. Hooray!

The verb doesn't change

There is no need to learn different grammatical forms of verbs (like in many European languages).

是　**to be** shì

我是　wǒ shì　**I am**

你是　nǐ shì　**you are**

他是　tā shì　**he is**

There is no change to the Chinese verb... but the English changes three times.

No past, no future

In Chinese there are no verb tenses. Here are two ways to change the tense:

1 Add context to a sentence with time words for example, 'next year', 'yesterday', or 'tomorrow'.

昨天　**yesterday** zuótiān

明天　**tomorrow** míngtiān

2 You can show an action has been completed by adding the little word 'le' after the verb or at the end of the sentence.

了　le

我昨天去了。	Wǒ zuótiān qù le.	I *went* yesterday.
我明天去。	Wǒ míngtiān qù.	I *am going* tomorrow.
我去了。	Wǒ qù le.	I *went.*

See! The verb in Chinese, 'qù' (to go), doesn't change.

Note: the time comes BEFORE the verb in Chinese.

Singular and plural nouns

There is no difference between singular and plural nouns. In other words, there is no equivalent to the English '-s' or '-es' added to nouns.

| 马喜欢吃苹果 | Mǎ xǐhuan chī píngguǒ. | **Horses like eating apples.** |

The Chinese for this sentence literally means 'horse like eat apple'. As there is no particular horse being referred to, this is translated as a general statement. **CONTEXT** is important in Chinese.

In general

Chinese often uses fewer words and seems simpler. In fact, some of the expressions used in English that have come directly from Chinese highlight the simple grammar constructions:

long time no see	hǎo jiǔ bù jiàn	好久不见
look-see	kàn kan	看看
no can do	bù néng zuò	不能做
no-go	bù qù	不去

First words

track 7

What are the first words to learn in any language? These ones of course!

你好

nǐ hǎo

hello

再见

zàijiàn

goodbye

谢谢

xièxie

thank you

对不起

duìbuqǐ

sorry

And this phrase may be useful too!

 **Where's the toilet?**

厕所在哪儿?

cèsuǒ zài nǎr?

男 nán **gents**

女 nǚ **ladies**

Where is...?　　zài nǎr?

Simply add '**zài nǎr?**' AFTER any noun to ask where something is:

'**Fàndiàn**' means **restaurant**.

'**Fàndiàn zài nǎr?**' means '**Where's the restaurant?**'

New words　生词

你好	nǐ hǎo	**hello**
再见	zaìjiàn	**goodbye**
谢谢	xièxie	**thank you**
对不起	duìbuqǐ	**sorry**
厕所	cèsuǒ	**toilet**
在哪儿	... zài nǎr?	**where is...?**

Welcome!

Chinese people are very hospitable. When you visit, they will welcome you and offer you a drink. The drink of choice is often tea.

请进！ **Please come in.**

Qǐng jìn!

请坐！ **Please sit down.**

Qǐng zuò!

请喝茶！ **Please have a cup of tea.**

Qǐng hē chá!

qǐng

This word means 'please' and you always put it at the beginning of sentences in Chinese.

These two characters mean 'new words' and are pronounced 'shēngcí'

↓

生词

New words

请	qǐng	**please**
进	jìn	**to enter**
坐	zuò	**to sit**
喝	hē	**to drink**
茶	chá	**tea**

In China, tea is the national drink. There are many different types with two popular varieties being black tea and green tea. Chinese people don't add milk to their tea.

How do you do?

When you meet Chinese people, greet them and introduce yourself in Chinese to set a good impression.

How are you?

你好吗?

Nǐ hǎo ma?

I'm very well.

我很好。

Wǒ hěn hǎo.

> Two third tones in a row are difficult to say. Where this happens, the first one is said as a second tone. Nǐ hǎo **changes to** Ní hǎo

> Wǒ hěn hǎo **changes to** Wó hén hǎo

生词

New words

我	wǒ	**I**	叫	jiào	**to be called**
你	nǐ	**you**	什么	shénme	**what**
很	hěn	**very**	吗	ma	**[question particle]** see page 80
好	hǎo	**good**			

What's your name?

你叫什么？

Nǐ jiào shénme?

I'm called Wang Ying.

我叫王英。

Wǒ jiào Wáng Yīng.

This is a Chinese full stop.

A Chinese name for you

Not all English names can be easily pronounced in China, so it is a good idea for you to have a Chinese name. Generally a Chinese teacher or Chinese friend can help you choose one, and this is the best way to get one. There are also websites that can give you a name. This is a good one:

http://www.mandarintools.com/chinesename.html

👤🎧 Chinese names

Chinese names all have a meaning. They start with the family name, then the given names follow. Chinese people either have one or two given names.

	Yáo Míng	Gǒng Lì	Jackie Chan

Surname ▶	Yáo	Gǒng	—
Given name(s) ▶	Míng	Lì	Chéng Lóng
Meaning of given name ▶	Bright	Clever	Successful Dragon

This is his stage name.

Addressing Chinese people

Adults should always be addressed by their full name (surname, given name), or with a title, which comes AFTER the surname, for example:

先生 xiānsheng **Mr**
eg Wáng xiānsheng

老师 lǎoshī **teacher**
eg Liú lǎoshī

Jackie Chan's mother called him 'Pao Pao', meaning 'cannonball', when he was a baby.

Children or friends can be addressed by their given names, or if the person is a very good friend or family, by their nickname. Chinese people often have a nickname.

The family name

The majority of the population of China have one of just 20 surnames. Here's a list of the top five.

1 Lǐ
2 Wáng
3 Zhāng
4 Liú
5 Chén

xìng
surname

Given names

As for first names, parents can choose from thousands of characters. Here are some popular girls' and boys' names:

Girls 1 Yīng (talented, wise)
2 Xiù (elegant, beautiful)
3 Yù (jade)
4 Huá (brilliant)
5 Zhēn (precious)

Boys 1 Wén (culture, writing)
2 Míng (bright)
3 Guó (nation)
4 Huá (brilliant)
5 Dé (virtue)

míng
given name(s)

Taboo!
Chinese people never call their children after anyone else.

Conversation practice 1

Test yourself on what you have learnt in this section.

Q. Can you translate this conversation into Chinese?

❶ Hello.

❷ Hello.

❸ How are you?

❹ I'm very well.

❺ Goodbye.

❻ Goodbye.

A. Here it is in Chinese.

❶ 你好！   Nǐ hǎo!

❷ 你好！   Nǐ hǎo!

❸ 你好吗？ Nǐ hǎo ma?

❹ 我很好！ Wǒ hěn hǎo!

❺ 再见！   Zàijiàn!

❻ 再见！   Zàijiàn!

Q. **Can you translate these phrases into Chinese?**

❶ Where's the toilet?

❷ Sit down, please.

❸ Please come in.

❹ What's your name?

❺ I am called...

A. **Here are the correct translations.**

❶ 厕所在哪儿？
Cèsuǒ zài nǎr?

❷ 请坐！
Qǐng zuò!

❸ 请进！
Qǐng jìn!

❹ 你叫什么？
Nǐ jiào shénme?

❺ 我叫……
Wǒ jiào...

Where are you from?

track 12

Find out how to say where you come from. This is one of the first questions you are asked in China.

你是哪国人?

Nǐ shì nǎ guó rén?
Which country are you from?

我是英国人。

Wǒ shì Yīngguórén.
I'm British.

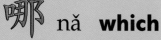 nǎ **which**

Here is the 'question word' 哪. 'Nǐ shì nǎ guó rén?' literally means 'You are which country person?'

人 rén **person**

By adding 'rén' to any of the country's names, you are saying 'people or person' of the country.

Countries

The characters for the country names are a mixture of how the word sounds (phonetic) and meaning.

🇺🇸	美国	Měiguó	**USA (beautiful country)**
	泰国	Tàiguó	**Thailand (tranquil country)**
🇬🇧	英国	Yīngguó	**Britain (brave country)**
	法国	Fǎguó	**France (legal country)**
	德国	Déguó	**Germany (virtuous country)**
	中国	Zhōngguó	**China (middle country)**
	日本	Rìběn	**Japan (rising sun)**
	加拿大	Jiānádà	**Canada (phonetic)**
	澳大利亚	Àodàlìyà	**Australia (phonetic)**
	荷兰	Hélán	**The Netherlands (phonetic – Holland)**

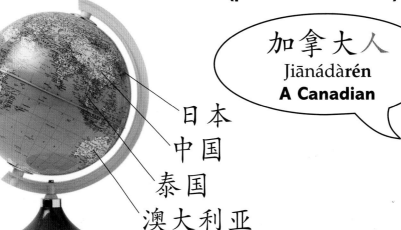

加拿大人
Jiānádà**rén**
A Canadian

日本
中国
泰国
澳大利亚

人

My body

Head, shoulders, knees, and toes...

耳朵	ěrduo	**ear**
眼睛	yǎnjing	**eye**
嘴巴	zuǐba	**mouth**
鼻子	bízi	**nose**
头	tóu	**head**
头发	tóufa	**hair**
手	shǒu	**hand**
脚	jiǎo	**foot**
肚子	dùzi	**stomach**
腿	tuǐ	**leg**
胳膊	gēbo	**arm**

44 All About Me

脚

... knees and toes...

腿

肚子

胳膊

嘴巴

鼻子

耳朵

眼睛

头

头发

手

Face facts

This head shows how you can play with characters to help you to remember them. (The parts of the characters used to make the features on this face are pictographs.)

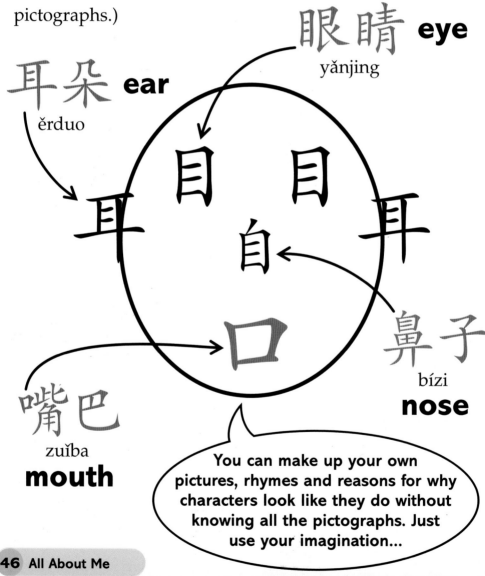

眼睛 **eye**
yǎnjing

耳朵 **ear**
ěrduo

鼻子
bízi
nose

嘴巴
zuǐba
mouth

You can make up your own pictures, rhymes and reasons for why characters look like they do without knowing all the pictographs. Just use your imagination...

big

Use the words for 'big' and 'small' to describe your facial features.

small

小

xiǎo

大

dà

我的耳朵大。Wǒ de ěrduo dà. **My ears are big.**

我的鼻子小。Wǒ de bízi xiǎo. **My nose is small.**

的 'de' is a new word – see page 49 for what it is.

Family and friends

In Chinese, there are words to describe what position you are in the family. For example, 'younger sister' is 'mèimei'.

妹妹 mèimei
younger sister

弟弟 dìdi
younger brother

姐姐 jiějie
older sister

哥哥 gēge
older brother

爸爸 bàba
father

妈妈 māma
mother

祖母 zǔmǔ
grandmother

祖父 zǔfù
grandfather

Making introductions

Use these words to make introductions.

生词

New words

这是	zhè shì	**This is...**
老师	lǎoshī	**teacher**
朋友	péngyou	**friend**
的	de	**[possessive particle]**

这是我的老师。

Zhè shì wǒ de lǎoshī.   **This is my teacher.**

If you are introducing a friend or family, you can miss out the 'de':

这是我朋友。

My, your, his, her

的 (de) is the most common character in Chinese. Here it is used to make 'I' into 'my'. And so on...

的

我 的 wǒ de **my**

你 的 nǐ de **your**

他 的 tā de **his**

她 的 tā de **her**

'His' and 'her' sound the same but have different characters.

Respect!

Confucianism is the name of the philosophy that has shaped Chinese culture since around 300 BCE. And when it comes to families, Confucianism is all about respect.

xiào
filial piety

Family lore

'Filial piety' is considered one of the greatest virtues of Confucianism. It means, in general terms, love and respect for parents and ancestors.

Confucius says...

Here are some of Confucius's rules for filial piety:

1 Take care of your parents
2 Don't be rebellious
3 Show love, respect, and support
4 Display courtesy
5 Uphold fraternity among brothers
6 Wisely advise your parents
7 Carry out sacrifices after their death

Kǒng fūzǐ   **Confucius**

Confucius was born in c.551 BCE and was a social philosopher whose teachings have influenced East Asian life for 2000 years.

The Confucian hierarchy within families means that fa
ower down in the hierarchy show filial piety to those
Grandad is top dog, and littlest sister is on the bottom

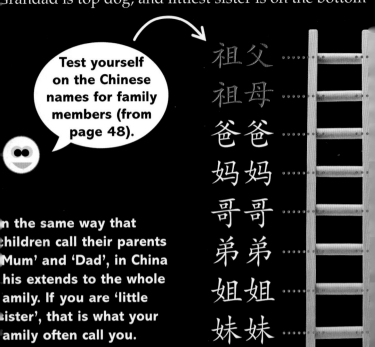

Test yourself on the Chinese names for family members (from page 48).

祖父 ......
祖母 ......
爸爸 ......
妈妈 ......
哥哥 ......
弟弟 ......
姐姐 ......
妹妹 ......

In the same way that children call their parents 'Mum' and 'Dad', in China this extends to the whole family. If you are 'little sister', that is what your family often call you.

Ancestor worship

Although these rules were set more than 2000 years ag
Confucian beliefs are ingrained into Chinese culture ar
family relationships to the present day. One of the mos
noticeable aspects is ancestor worship.

Ancestor worship includes burning incense and making offerings to the deceased of food and other things, even a toothbrush and slippers, to use in the afterlife.

Conversation practice 2

Test yourself on what you have learnt in this section.

Q. Can you translate this conversation into Chinese?

1 Where do you come from?
2 I'm British.
3 This is my teacher.
4 She is Chinese.

A. Here it is in Chinese.

1 你是哪国人?
Nǐ shì nǎ guó rén?

2 我是英国人。
Wǒ shì Yīngguórén.

3 这是我的老师。
Zhè shì wǒ de lǎoshī.

4 她是中国人。
Tā shì Zhōngguórén.

Q.

Can you translate these phrases into Chinese?

❶ I am American.

❷ She is Canadian.

❸ This is my friend.

❹ This is her younger sister.

❺ This is his older brother.

A.

Here are the correct translations.

❶ 我是美国人。
Wǒ shì Měiguórén.

❷ 她是加拿大人。
Tā shì Jiānádàrén.

❸ 这是我朋友。
Zhè shì wǒ péngyou.

❹ 这是她的妹妹。
Zhè shì tā de mèimei.

❺ 这是他的哥哥。
Zhè shì tā de gēge.

Numbers 1–10

track 17

Learning numbers 1–10

is one of the most useful and simple lessons of Chinese. Once you know them, you will be able to:

- count higher
- say the date
- learn the vocabulary for the months of the year...
- ... and the days of the week
- tell the time
- find out the cost of things

shùzì

number

Writing numbers

When you write numbers, imagine you are writing on a grid of equal-sized squares. Remember to write strokes from top to bottom, and left to right.

1 一 yī **one**

2 二 èr **two**

3 三 sān **three**

4 四 sì **four**

5 五 wǔ **five**

6 六 liù **six**

7 七 qī **seven**

8 八 bā **eight**

9 九 jiǔ **nine**

10 十 shí **ten**

It's simple maths

To count from 10–99, you build on the numbers 1–10. There are two simple rules to follow:

- If a number comes *after* 10 (十), you *add* it to 10.
- If a number comes *before* 10 (十), you *times* it by 10.

How it works...

十二	shíèr	12	2 (二) *after* 10 (十), so that means 10 + 2
二十	èrshí	20	2 (二) *before* 10 (十), so that means 2 × 10
二十二	èrshíèr	22	2 (二) *after* and *before* 10 (十), so that means (2 × 10) + 2

Q. What are these numbers?

1 三十 3 四十五

2 十六 4 七十八

A. 1. 30; 2. 16; 3. 45; 4. 78

100 plus

The same rule applies when you go over 100. But, before you can do that, you need to know these words.

New words 生词		
百	bǎi	**100**
千	qiān	**1,000**
万	wàn	**10,000**
百万	bǎiwàn	**1,000,000**

How it works

The larger numbers string together in much the same way, with the above words for 10, 100, 1,000 etc. acting as 'stops'.

三百五十
sānbǎiwǔshí
(3×100) + (5×10) = 350

五千四百
wǔqiānsìbǎi
(5×1000) + (4×100) = 5,400

六万
liùwàn
6 × 10,000 = 60,000

七百万
qībǎiwàn
7 × 1,000,000 = 7,000,000

Number rules

track 19

There are a couple of things about numbers it is worth pointing out now.

Measure words

In Chinese, you need a measure word between a number and a noun. You can't just say 'one person', you have to say 'one **something of** person'. Most Chinese measure words have no direct translation into English although the concept is similar to 'two **plots** of land', 'two **pinches** of salt', 'four **head** of cattle'.

个 ge
The toneless 'ge' is by far the most common measure word. You can use this for most things. If in doubt use 'ge'.

Number	Measure	Noun	Meaning
五 wǔ	个 ge	人 rén	**five people**
三 sān	个 ge	光盘 guāngpán	**three CDs**

本 běn
'Běn' is the measure word used for books. Try to remember this one too.

五 wǔ	本 běn	书 shū	**five books**

Tricksy number two

The number two is, err, 'èr' – we know that. However, if we are saying 'two of something', we say 'liǎng' instead of 'èr'.

两 liǎng
two

两个纪念品
liǎng ge jìniànpǐn
Two souvenirs

两个自行车
liǎng ge zìxíngchē
Two bicycles

Q. Say how many there are of each thing

Use a measure word and 'liǎng' where necessary.

1 shū **books**

2 péngyou **friends**

A. 1. liǎng běn shū; 2. sān ge péngyou

What's the date?

In Chinese, you use numbers to say the days of the week and months of the year.

Days of the week

1 星期一 **Monday** ☎
xīngqīyī
phone dentist

2 星期二 **Tuesday**
xīngqīèr

3 星期三 **Wednesday**
xīngqīsān

4 星期四 **Thursday** ✉
xīngqīsì
post birthday card

5 星期五 **Friday**
xīngqīwǔ

6 星期六 **Saturday**
xīngqīliù
go on holiday! ✈

7 星期天 **Sunday**
xīngqītiān

Only Sunday is different – a day off numbers.

生词

New words

年 nián **year**

月 yuè **month**

号 hào **date**

零 líng **zero**

To make a year date, you simply put the number of the year before 'nián' eg, 2007 is 2007 'nián'.

To make a day date, you put the number of the day before 'hào' eg, 25th is 25 'hào'.

Months of the year

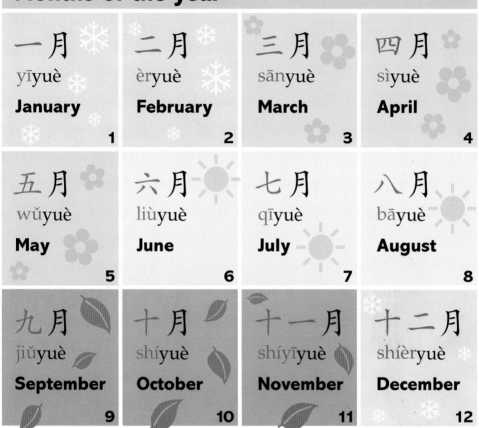

一月 yīyuè
January
1

二月 èryuè
February
2

三月 sānyuè
March
3

四月 sìyuè
April
4

五月 wǔyuè
May
5

六月 liùyuè
June
6

七月 qīyuè
July
7

八月 bāyuè
August
8

九月 jiǔyuè
September
9

十月 shíyuè
October
10

十一月 shíyīyuè
November
11

十二月 shíèryuè
December
12

Now make a date

In Chinese, the year goes first, then the month, then the day. This follows a general grammatical rule of Chinese: **'least specific, to most specific.'**

Wednesday, 3rd October 2007

二零零七年， 十月， 三号， 星期三

èrlínglíngqī nián,   shíyuè,   sānhào,   xīngqīsān

2007   **October**   **3rd**   **Wednesday**

Birthday party

Traditionally, Chinese people have not made a big deal about birthdays. Nowadays, especially in the cities, they celebrate them with a cake and a party.

生日快乐!

Shēngri kuàilè!

Happy birthday!

Two ages

Chinese people may have two ages – one from the traditional age system, and one from the Western age system.

Two years old

The traditional way of counting a person's age is that newborns start at one year old, and one year is added at each Chinese new year (which follows the lunar calendar). This explains why Chinese babies can be said to be 'two years old' when they are still tiny.

How old are you?

There are two ways of asking this question in Chinese:

1 你几岁了？

Nǐ jǐ suì le?

How old are you?

Use this when you are addressing a child under 10.

2 你多大了？

Nǐ duō dà le?

How old are you?

Use this for adults and children.

To answer the question, you say:

我 xx 岁 。 Wǒ xx suì. **I'm xx years old.**

Birthday food

Many people like to eat 'longevity noodles', symbols of long life inspired by the noodle's shape. Many people choose to eat Western-style birthday cakes too.

Signs of the

Are you a rat, a pig, or a dragon?

鼠　牛　虎　兔　龙　蛇

RAT	OX	TIGER	RABBIT	DRAGON	SNAKE
1912	1913	1914	1915	1916	1917
1924	1925	1926	1927	1928	1929
1936	1937	1938	1939	1940	1941
1948	1949	1950	1951	1952	1953
1960	1961	1962	1963	1964	1965
1972	1973	1974	1975	1976	1977
1984	1985	1986	1987	1988	1989
1996	1997	1998	1999	2000	2001
2008	2009	2010	2011	2012	2013

Zodiac

Each year starts in late January/February depending on the moon's cycle. If you are born in January, you may fall into the previous year.

The year you were born determines your sign of the zodiac in Chinese astrology. Look up your sign and then find out what you're like on the next page...

HORSE	SHEEP	MONKEY	ROOSTER	DOG	PIG
1918	1919	1920	1921	1922	1923
1930	1931	1932	1933	1934	1935
1942	1943	1944	1945	1946	1947
1954	1955	1956	1957	1958	1959
1966	1967	1968	1969	1970	1971
1978	1979	1980	1981	1982	1983
1990	1991	1992	1993	1994	1995
2002	2003	2004	2005	2006	2007
2014	2015	2016	2017	2018	2019

rat
shǔ

Rats are charming, quick-witted, and make loyal friends – once you let people get to know you. You are organised and honest, and you prefer to live under your own rules.

 ## ox
niú

You are a born leader, and inspire confidence in all who know you. Being conservative and methodical you find it hard to let your hair down, but you are good at most things you turn your hand to.

 ## tiger
hǔ

Tigers are born leaders. You are often respected for your courage and you are good at standing up for what you believe in. However, you need to guard against being too bossy!

 ## rabbit
tù

You are a warm, cosy type of person, affectionate and obliging. However, you get too sentimental and can seem superficial. Being cautious and conservative, you make a good negotiator and you are the first to sort out rows.

 ## dragon
lóng

You are full of life – enthusiastic and popular. You are intelligent, gifted, and a perfectionist but these qualities can make you intolerant of others. Watch out for being too sharp with people.

 ## snake
shé

Wise, charming, and romantic, you are a deep thinker and full of intuition. Avoid being stingy with money and always strive to keep your sense of humour about life.

horse
mǎ

You are very hard-working and independent. You are not easily led and are intelligent and friendly. You can be prone to showing off, but you are generally well-liked by everyone.

sheep
yáng

Except for the knack of putting your foot in it, the sheep is excellent company. You are elegant and artistic, but can be viewed as a bit of a whinger, so try not to complain too much!

monkey
hóu

Witty and intellligent, you have a magnetic personality, and are always well-liked. The monkey, however, must guard against being an opportunist and finds it hard to trust other people.

rooster
jī

The rooster is hard-working, shrewd, and good at making decisions. You speak your mind. You like looking good, and can be extravagant sometimes. Watch out for seeming boastful.

dog
gǒu

Dogs make very loyal, faithful, and honest friends – a dog will never let you down. You are a worrier though, and over-critical, but your bark is worse than your bite.

pig
zhū

You are always good company, an intellectual with a strong sense of purpose. You are sincere and honest, but because you expect the same from others, you can be naive.

Conversation practice 3

Test yourself on what you have learnt in this section.

Q. **Can you translate this conversation into Chinese?**

① **Happy birthday!**
② **Thank you!**
③ **How old are you?**
④ **I am 14.**

A. **Here it is in Chinese.**

① 生日快乐!
Shēngri kuàilè!

② 谢谢!
Xièxie!

③ 你多大了?
Nǐ duō dà le?

④ 我十四岁。
Wǒ shísì suì.

Q. **Can you translate these numbers and phrases into Chinese?**

❶ 54

❷ 2,500

❸ 29th May, 1971.

❹ 7 people

❺ 2 books

A. **Here are the correct translations.**

❶ 五十四
wǔshísì

❷ 二千五百
èrqiānwǔbǎi

❸ 一九七一年，五月
二十九号。
yījiǔqīyī nián, wǔyuè
èrshíjiǔ hào.

❹ 七个人
qī ge rén

❺ 两本书
liǎng běn shū

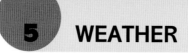

Seasons
track 23

China is the fourth biggest country in the world, only slightly smaller than the USA, and the climate in the south and north differs hugely.

The climate

In the south, it is sub-tropical and the land is fertile and green. In the northern winter, the temperature rarely rises above freezing, and basketball courts are turned into ice-skating rinks. Between the various extremes, the weather is continental and shows marked seasonal differences.

Nature puts on some dazzling seasonal displays in China, especially where the seasons are more extreme.

春天 chūntiān
spring

夏天 xiàtiān
summer

秋天 qiūtiān
autumn

冬天 dōngtiān
winter

🎧 Weather words

Talking about the weather is
an international ice-breaker.

Wow! It's hot!

There is a simple way to exclaim
about extreme weather conditions:

太热了！
Tài rè le!
It's boiling!

太冷了！
Tài lěng le!
It's freezing!

Using tài ... le

By using these two little words around a variety of adjectives
you can exclaim about things.

太大了！	Tài dà le!	**It's huge!**
太好了！	Tài hǎo le!	**That's great!**

Describing the weather

Here are the words for different types of weather.

 刮风 **windy**
gūa fēng

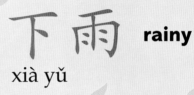 下雨 **rainy**
xià yǔ

热 **hot**
rè

 冷 **cold**
lěng

 下雪 **snowy**
xià xuě

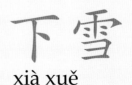

🎧 Vroom!

track 25

F rom crowded Beijing buses to express trains that zoom across China's vast countryside, every mode of transport is available in China.

To learn the words for different vehicles, first you need to know this general word:

车 chē **vehicle**

Breakdown

The table below shows how the meanings of the characters for vehicles break down. Try and guess the meanings of the words in the final column. Answers on the opposite page.

	Word	Pinyin	Meaning	New word
Add 'chē' 车:	自行	zìxíng	**by oneself**	自行车
	火	huǒ	**fire**	火车
	汽	qì	**vapour**	汽车
Add 'qìchē' 汽车:	公共	gōnggòng	**public**	公共汽车
	出租	chūzū	**for hire**	出租汽车
Put these together:	飞	fēi	**fly**	飞机
	机	jī	**machine**	

自行车
zìxíngchē
bicycle

火车
huǒchē
train

汽车
qìchē
car

公共汽车
gōnggòngqìchē
bus

出租汽车
chūzūqìchē
taxi

飞机
fēijī
aeroplane

Buying a ticket

You need to buy a ticket, the ticket seller doesn't speak English, and there is a queue of people behind you.

Don't panic!

New words 生词

想	xiǎng	**to want**	票	piào	**ticket**
买	mǎi	**to buy**	去	qù	**to go**

Station clock

Learn to say what time you need your ticket for.

Add diǎn to a number to say 'o'clock' and 'diǎn bàn' to say 'half past'.

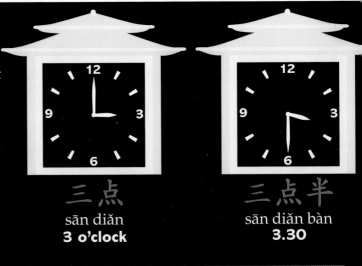

三点
sān diǎn
3 o'clock

三点半
sān diǎn bàn
3.30

New words 生词

几点	jǐ diǎn	**what time?**	分	fēn	**minute**
点	diǎn	**o'clock**	半	bàn	**half**

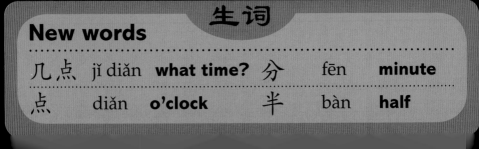

我想买票。去北京。

Wǒ xiǎng mǎi piào. Qù Běijīng.

I want to buy a ticket to Beijing.

Beijing Railway Station opened in the 1950s and merges traditional and fifties architecture.

Add however many fēn (minutes) to make other times

三点二十分
sān diǎn èrshí fēn
3.20

三点四十五分
sān diǎn sìshíwǔ fēn
3.45

Q. Look at the clock and answer the question in Chinese.

几点了？ **What time is it?**

Jǐ diǎn le?

A. 四点半 sì diǎn bàn 4.30

🎧 Asking the way

Even if you're in China with a tour group, you'll want to venture out on your own. Here's how to ask the way.

New words 生词

请问	qǐng wèn	**excuse me**
...在哪儿?	...zài nǎr?	**where is...?**
左边	zuǒbian	**left**
右边	yòubian	**right**
一直走	yīzhí zǒu	**straight on**
然后	ránhòu	**then, afterwards**
茶馆	cháguǎn	**teahouse**
饭店	fàndiàn	**restaurant**

停
tíng
stop

Practice time

Find the teahouse by following the instructions for the red trail.

请问，
Qǐng wèn,

茶馆在哪儿？
cháguǎn zài nǎr?

转
zhuǎn
to turn

一直走。
Yīzhí zǒu.

然后右转，然后左转。
Ránhòu yòu zhuǎn, ránhòu zuǒ zhuǎn.

茶馆在右边。
Cháguǎn zài yòubian.

茶馆 cháguǎn
tea house

茶馆

饭店

Q. Give directions...

Now give directions yourself, for the man to follow the blue trail to the restaurant.

饭店
fàndiàn
restaurant

A. 右边。然后一直走，然后右左转。饭店在左边。
Yòubiān. Ránhòu yīzhí zǒu, ránhòu zuǒzhuǎn. Fàndiàn zài zuǒbiān.
Right, then straight on, then left. The restaurant is on the left.

🎧 Questions

Here are two ways to ask a question in Chinese.

1. 'ma'

The little word 'ma' 吗 is all you need to make questions. Simply add it to a statement, and it makes the statement into a question.

他去北京。
Tā qù Běijīng.

He is going to Beijing.

他去北京吗？
Tā qù Běijīng ma?

Is he going to Beijing?

汽车站在左边。
Qìchēzhàn zài zuǒbian.

The bus stop is on the left.

汽车站在左边吗？
Qìchēzhàn zài zuǒbian ma?

Is the bus stop on the left?

Q. Turn this statement into a question.

公共汽车去北京。
Gōnggòngqìchē qù Běijīng.
The bus is going to Beijing.

A. 公共汽车去北京吗？ Gōnggòngqìchē qù Běijīng ma! **Is the bus going to Beijing?**

2. Boo!

That's not a Chinese word, but it sounds like one: 'bù' 不, meaning 'not' or 'no'. If you put 'bù' between two repeated words, (eg. 'qù' 去 meaning 'to go') it makes a question.

你去不去? Nǐ qù bù qù? **Are you going?**

> Chinese doesn't have words for 'yes' and 'no'. This is a way of saying 'yes' or 'no' too.

And you answer the question by repeating the verb.

去。 **I'm going. /Yes.**
Qù.

不去。 **I'm not going. /No.**
Bù qù.

Q. Answer this question (using 'mǎi' 买 meaning 'to buy').

你买不买? **Are you going to buy it?**
Nǐ mǎi bù mǎi?

The exception

You don't use 'bù' between the verb for 'to have', which is 'yǒu' (pronounced 'yǒ'). Instead you use 'méi' 没 to make the negative.

有没有? Yǒu méi yǒu? **Have you got one?**

有。 Yǒu. **I have one. /Yes**

没有。 Méi yǒu. **I haven't got one. /No**

A. 买 · mǎi. **Yes.** 不买 · bù mǎi. **No.**

Getting around

China has the third largest rail network in the world, the most bicyclists, more aeroplanes taking off by the day, and a fast evolving network of roads.

Bicycles

There are 300 million bicycles being ridden around in China – 33 bikes to every one car. Bike sales are decreasing however, as more and more people can afford cars.

The pedicab

The famous rickshaw has been phased out in China, and replaced by the pedicab.

Traffic

The traffic in Beijing and many other Chinese cities is congested and slow-moving. Trucks, buses, cars, taxis, bicycles, pedicabs, and minibuses clog the roads.

堵车   dǔchē
traffic jam

Hard seat – the seats are upholstered but they are cramped and uncomfortable. This is the cheapest option.

Hard-sleeper – these carriages are made up of door-less compartments. Each one contains six beds in three tiers. Hard sleeper tickets are the first to sell out for long journeys.

硬座
yìngzuò

硬卧
yìngwò

By train
For visitors, train travel provides a great opportunity to meet Chinese people as well as take in the beautiful scenery. There are four different levels of seating in Chinese trains.

Soft seat – these comfortable seats have lots of leg-room and are ideal for relatively short journeys.

Soft-sleeper – this is the most luxurious option. The beds are comfortable, with four per compartment. It is also the most expensive choice.

软座 ruǎnzuò

软卧 ruǎnwò

track 29

Conversation practice 4

Test yourself on what you have learnt in this section.

Q. **Can you translate this conversation into Chinese?**

❶ I would like to buy a ticket to Beijing.

❷ What time are you going?

❸ Four o'clock.

❹ That's fine.

A. **Here it is in Chinese.**

❶ 我想买票去北京。
Wǒ xiǎng mǎi piào qù Běijīng.

❷ 你几点去？
Nǐ jǐ diǎn qù?

❸ 四点。
Sì diǎn.

❹ 好了。
Hǎo le.

Q. Can you translate these into Chinese?

❶ Excuse me.

❷ Go straight ahead.

❸ Are you going?

❹ What time is it?

❺ 6.45.

A. Here are the correct translations.

❶ 请问。
Qǐng wèn.

❷ 一直走。
Yīzhí zǒu.

❸ 你去不去？/ 你去吗？
Nǐ qù bù qù?/ Nǐ qù ma?

❹ 几点了？
Jǐ diǎn le?

❺ 六点四十五分 。
Liù diǎn sìshíwǔ fēn.

 Place settings

Chinese place settings can confuse a foreigner, and the other way around. So here's a rough guide.

叉
chā
fork

刀
dāo
knife

pánzi
plate

刀叉 dāo-chā **knife and fork**

Hard or easy? 用筷子很难。

难
nán **hard**

Yòng kuàizi hěn nán.
Using chopsticks is hard.

Chinese style

You use chopsticks to take bite-size morsels of food from a selection of different dishes. The bowl often holds plain rice, which you also eat with chopsticks. You use the spoon to eat soup.

碗
wǎn
bowl

筷子
kuàizi
chopsticks

勺子
sháozi
spoon

容易
róngyì **easy**

用筷子很容易。
Yòng kuàizi hěn róngyì.
Using chopsticks is easy.

Don't flip the fish!

Chinese people are masters at making you feel welcome. And a meal is a favourite way to show hospitality. Follow this guide to etiquette so you know the do's and don'ts of a meal in China.

❦ *Etiquette* ❦

Burp!

Never start before your host says so. And don't be surprised if your host continuously urges you to try each dish – (s)he is making sure you are taken care of, not pressurizing you.

Compliment the host on how good the food is. Just like at home, this will please your host. Also, be bold and say with conviction 'I am happy to make good friends' or 'I feel very welcome'.

Don't flip over a fish to eat the meat on the other side. This is because Chinese people believe turning a fish resembles a boat capsizing.

Avoid stuffing yourself then suddenly stopping. It's best to gradually stop eating. Leave a little food and drink – this means that you are satisfied and that the host has provided ample food.

Slurp!

Do pour drinks for people sitting next to you.

Ignore slurps, burps and other meal-time noises – these are considered sounds of appreciation.

Table plan

Tables are often round. The seating is arranged in order of status. The host sits facing the door, with guest 1 on his right, and guest 2 on his left. The co-host usually sits nearest to the door with guests 3 and 4 around him or her. Status is often decided in order of age.

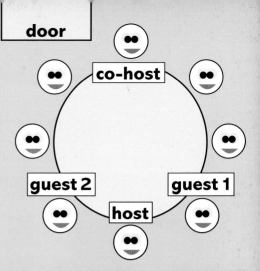

door

co-host

guest 2

guest 1

host

Chopstick no-nos

- Don't dig in the food on a plate but just pick up the piece that you want.
- Don't let your chopsticks be covered with food juice or residue.
- Don't spear things with your chopsticks.
- Don't put chopsticks vertically in rice in a bowl since it resembles the incense sticks for the dead.

How to hold chopsticks

Useful phrases

...to try out at your next Chinese meal.

我自己来	wǒ zìjǐ lái	**I'll help myself**
我吃饱了	wǒ chī bǎo le	**I'm full**
很好吃	hěn hǎo chī	**It's delicious!**

track 31

⬤ Live to eat!

This is a popular saying in southern China – and Chinese food is succulent and incredibly varied. Here are some 'foody' words, just for starters.

米饭
mǐfàn
rice

面条
miàntiáo
noodles

肉 ròu
meat

鸡 jī
chicken

鱼 yú
fish

(烤)鸭
(kǎo) yā
(roast) duck

矿泉水
kuàngquánshuǐ
mineral water

茶
chá
tea

果汁
guǒzhī
fruit juice

And some drinks.

点心
diǎnxīn
dim sum

饺子
jiǎozi
dumplings

蔬菜
shūcài
vegetables

水果
shuǐguǒ
fruit

我吃素
Wǒ chī sù.
I'm vegetarian.

🎧 At a restaurant

Next time you're in a Chinese restaurant, try impressing everyone by ordering the food in Chinese.

New words 生词

想	xiǎng	**to want**
服务员	fúwùyuán	**waiter/waitress**
买单	mǎidān	**the bill**
吃	chī	**to eat**
什么	shénme	**what**
菜单	càidān	**menu**
给	gěi	**to give**
饭店	fàndiàn	**restaurant**

在饭店
zài fàndiàn
at a restaurant

Many Beijing restaurants are pretty sophisticated. All over China, though, you can find noisy and informal restaurants that are great fun for a bite to eat.

Waiter. Please can I have the menu?

服务员。请给我菜单。

Fúwùyuán. Qǐng gěi wǒ càidān.

这是菜单。

Zhè shì càidān.

你想吃什么?

Nǐ xiǎng chī shénme?

Here's the menu. What would you like?

I would like some dumplings.

我想吃饺子。

Wǒ xiǎng chī jiǎozi.

That was delicious.

很好吃。

Hěn hǎo chī.

Please can I have the bill?

请给我买单。

Qǐng gěi wǒ mǎidān.

Conversation practice 5

Test yourself on what you have learnt in this section.

Q. **Can you translate this conversation into Chinese?**

❶ Waiter!
❷ Hello. What would you like to eat?
❸ I'd like some noodles.
❹ OK.
❺ Thank you. These are delicious!

A. **Here it is in Chinese.**

❶ 服务员！Fúwùyuán!

❷ 你好。你想吃什么？
Nǐ hǎo. Nǐ xiǎng chī shénme?

❸ 我想要面条。
Wǒ xiǎngyào miàntiáo.

❹ 好。Hǎo.

❺ 谢谢 。很好吃。
Xièxie. Hěn hǎo chī.

Q. **Can you translate these into Chinese?**

❶ I'm vegetarian.

❷ I'll help myself.

❸ I'm full.

❹ Using chopsticks is hard.

❺ Using chopsticks is easy.

A. **Here are the correct translations.**

❶ 我吃素。
Wǒ chī sù.

❷ 我自己来。
Wǒ zìjǐ lái.

❸ 我吃饱了。
Wǒ chī bǎo le.

❹ 用筷子很难。
Yòng kuàizi hěn nán.

❺ 用筷子很 容易。
Yòng kuàizi hěn róngyì.

Fun and games

track 35

A<small>PART FROM</small> learning Chinese, you may have other hobbies. Look down this list of popular pastimes and choose some you enjoy.

网球
wǎngqiú
tennis

足球
zúqiú
football

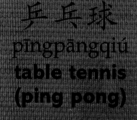

乒乓球
pīngpāngqiú
**table tennis
(ping pong)**

球
qiú
ball

滑板
huábǎn
skate boarding

听音乐
tīng yīnyuè
listening to music

看书
kàn shū
reading

学习中文
xuéxí Zhōngwén
learning Chinese

很好玩儿!
hěn hǎo wánr!
great fun!

画画
huàhuà
painting

游泳
yóuyǒng
swimming

滑冰
huábīng
iceskating

滑雪
huáxuě
skiing

track 36

Find a Chinese speaking friend if you can and practise chatting about things you like, love, and don't like.

New words	生词	
喜欢	xǐhuan	**to like**
爱	ài	**to love**
打	dǎ	**to play**
也	yě	**also / too**
你呢？	nǐ ne?	**how about you?**

I like...

我喜欢打网球。
Wǒ xǐhuan dǎ wǎngqíu.
I like tennis.

You add 'bù' 不 before the verb to make a sentence negative.

I don't like...

我不喜欢打网球。
Wǒ bù xǐhuan dǎ wǎngqíu.
I don't like tennis.

I also like...

To say that you 'also' like something else, you slip 'yě' 也 in before the verb.

我也喜欢滑板。

Wǒ yě xǐhuan huábǎn.

I like skateboarding too.

我也喜欢听音乐。

Wǒ yě xǐhuan tīng yīnyuè.

I like listening to music too.

How about you?

If you want to ask someone else if they like something, you simply say 'nǐ ne?' 你呢?

我喜欢打网球。你呢?

Wǒ xǐhuan dǎ wǎngqíu. Nǐ ne?

I like tennis. How about you?

我爱你

Wǒ ài nǐ.

If you like nothing more than another person, here's how to say 'I love you' in Chinese.

Ping pong and Mahjong

track 37

Traditional pastimes are alive and kicking all over China.

Martial arts

Many different forms of martial art have developed over the past 2,000 years and the styles are quite distinctive. Each style offers self-defence, improved health, and self-cultivation.

At 6am in Shanghai, many people start the day with tai chi.

太极拳 tàijíquán
Tai chi

Ping pong

Ping pong is one of the biggest sports in China today, played by an estimated 200 million players. The ping pong tables in village squares are a popular place to hang out and practise, and maybe dream of one day becoming an Olympic star...

A general term for Chinese martial arts:

武术 wǔshù

乒乓球
pīngpāngqiú

Mahjong

Mahjong is as popular as ever in China. The game has complex rules and can turn into marathon sessions! It is always accompanied by a loud 'click-clacking' noise as the tiles knock against each other.

麻将　　májiàng

Chinese chess

Xiàngqí (Chinese chess) is one of the most popular board games in China. This highly strategic game was played as early as the 4th century BCE and is similar to chess played in the West; a real mental battle.

象棋　　xiàngqí

Chinese Opera

Chinese Opera is more than a thousand years old. Instruments accompany the acting, which is based on gestures and footwork to express actions such as riding a horse or opening a door. The actors' elaborate make-up defines their roles.

Jīngjù
**Beijing Opera
(one of many
different forms)**

What's hot?

What's hot in China today? Kids are doing the same thing from Times Square to Tiananmen Square.

Shanghai

Shanghai is China's city of dreams. Full of new ideas and cutting-edge culture, it is the fastest growing city in the world. A 24-hour city, Shanghai is wide awake at every hour. It seethes with energy and noise.

上海

Shànghǎi
Shanghai

Olympics

The 2008 Olympics to be held in Beijing will bring Chinese national pride to fever pitch. It is set to start at 8 o'clock, on the 8th August, 2008 – 8 is a lucky number in China.

奥运会 Àoyùnhuì
Olympics

The internet

The internet is hot! Blogs, podcasts, sms, music downloads... 100 million people are net users but there are relatively few home computers. People meet up with friends at their local internet cafe.

上网 shàng wǎng
surfing the net

Tourism

Chinese people are travelling in ever-increasing numbers around their own country and abroad.

一路平安！
yí lù píng'ān
Have a good trip!

Pop idol

As in the West, Chinese kids love pop music. 'Cantopop' is the name of a popular genre. They also listen to rap, heavy metal, and punk music. A Chinese version of 'Pop Idol' (called 'Supergirl Contest') has been a recent huge hit – with 400 million viewers.

Li Yuchun (centre) was the 21-year-old winner of the 'Supergirl Contest' in 2006.

Slang

track 39

Mandarin, like any language, is evolving. New slang is invented all the time, and words enter the language as foreign influence broadens. Here are some commonly used 'new' words.

Lots of these words have been adopted since 1978 following Deng Xiaoping's 'Open door policy'. There has been a period of economic reform since then, as China has opened up to Japan and the West.

Exclamations!

酷 kù! **cool!**

拜拜 bái bái! **Bye!**

OK OK **OK!**

嗨 hài **hi/hey!**

Pastimes

蹦迪	bèngdí	**dance party**
上网聊天	shàngwǎng liáotiān	**online chatting**
卡拉OK	kǎlāOK	**karaoke**
瑜伽	yújiā	**yoga**
高尔夫球	gāo'ěrfūqiú	**golf**

Food

可乐	kělè **cola**
咖啡	kāfēi **coffee**
咖喱	gālí **curry**
派	pài **pie**
比萨	bǐsà **pizza**
汉堡	hànbǎo **hamburger**

Conversation practice 6

Test yourself on what you have learnt in this section.

Q. **Can you translate this conversation into Chinese?**

❶ I like swimming. How about you?

❷ I don't like swimming. I like football.

❸ I also like tennis.

❹ Tennis is good fun.

A. **Here it is in Chinese.**

❶ 我喜欢游泳。你呢?
Wǒ xǐhuan yóuyǒng. Nǐ ne?

❷ 我不喜欢游泳。
Wǒ bù xǐhuan yóuyǒng.

我喜欢足球。
Wǒ xǐhuan zúqiú.

❸ 我也喜欢网球。
Wǒ yě xǐhuan wǎngqiú.

❹ 网球很好玩儿 。
Wǎngqiú hěn hǎo wánr.

Q. Can you translate these phrases into Chinese?

❶ To learn Chinese
❷ Have a good trip!
❸ I love you.
❹ The Olympics
❺ Surfing the net

A. Here are the correct translations.

❶ 学习中文
xuéxí Zhōngwén

❷ 一路平安!
yī lù píng'ān!

❸ 我爱你!
Wǒ ài nǐ!

❹ 奥运会
Àoyùnhuì

❺ 上网
shàng wǎng

Beijing

track 41

There are many magnificent monuments
to see in China's cities, especially in the capital city, Beijing.

New words 生词		
看	kàn	**to see**
做	zuò	**to do**
长城	Chángchéng	**the Great Wall**
故宫	Gùgōng	**the Forbidden City**
天安门广场	Tiān'ānmén Guǎngchǎng	**Tiananmen Square**

What do you want to do in Beijing?

在北京你想做什么？

Zài Běijīng nǐ xiǎng zuò shénme?

我 想 看 ……

Wǒ xiǎng kàn...

I want to see...

长城

Chángchéng

the Great wall

故宫

Gùgōng

the Forbidden City

天安门广场

Tiān'ānmén Guǎngchǎng

Tiananmen Square

Some useful phrases

请你再说。

Qǐng nǐ zài shuō.

Please can you say it again.

我听不懂。

Wǒ tīng bù dǒng.

I don't understand.

你说英文吗？

Nǐ shuō yīngwén ma?

Do you speak English?

A day in the country

Whether you enjoy climbing mountains, hanging out at the beach, or cruising down a river, there is masses to see and do in China's countryside.

New words 生词

我们	wǒmen	**we**
上午	shàngwǔ	**morning**
下午	xiàwǔ	**afternoon**
爬	pá	**to climb**
山	shān	**mountain**
海边	hǎibiān	**seaside**
坐船	zuò chuán	**take a boat**
骑马	qí mǎ	**ride a horse**

This might help you remember the characters for 'morning' and 'afternoon'.

on
shàng
上 + 午 = morning

下 + = afternoon
xià   wǔ
under   **midday**

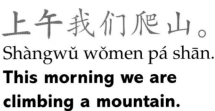

上午我们爬山。

Shàngwǔ wǒmen pá shān.

This morning we are climbing a mountain.

上午我们骑马。

Shàngwǔ wǒmen qí mǎ.

This morning we are going horse riding.

下午我们去海边。

Xiàwǔ wǒmen qù hǎibiān.

This afternoon we are going to the seaside.

下午我们坐船。

Xiàwǔ wǒmen zuò chuán.

This afternoon we are taking a boat.

track 43

At the market

Here are some of the things you can find in China's colourful and varied markets.

Make a sentence

Finish the sentence by choosing something to buy.

我去市场买......

Wǒ qù shìchǎng mǎi...

I'm going to the market to buy...

丝织品
sīzhīpǐn
silk

纪念品 jìniànpǐn
souvenirs

玉
yù
jade

工艺品
gōngyìpǐn
crafts

If you put the words for 'to buy' and 'to sell' next to each other, you get the word for 'business'.

买 + 卖 = 买卖
mǎi + mài = mǎimài
to buy + **to sell** = **business**

鞋子 xiézi
shoes

电器 diànqì
electrical goods

衣服 yīfu
clothes

陶瓷艺术
táocí yìshù
ceramics

书
shū
books

🎧 How to haggle

At a Chinese market you are expected to haggle.

It is part of buying something.

Two phrases

These two phrases are all you need for successful haggling.

How much is it?

多少钱?
duōshǎo qián?

It's too expensive!

太贵了!
tài guì le!

Chinese money

One unit of Chinese currency is a 'yuán'. People often say 'kuài' as well as 'yuán', which means the same thing.

A ten-yuan note

元
yuán

块
kuài

Haggling tips

Haggling is an art, and if you are good at it you can get good deals. It requires play-acting on both sides.

Sellers often have a large calculator which you can pass between you with your bids.

1) Look around the market and choose what you want to buy.

2) Ask the price. **duōshǎo qián?**

tài guì le!

3) If you think it is cheap, don't show it. Pretend you are surprised by how expensive it is. The initial price offered by the seller is usually AT LEAST 40% over the general price.

4) Throw out a low price, 1/5th of the one given by the seller. Have a big smile on your face when you say it. (Smiling always helps when haggling.)

5) The stall-holder may pretend to be cross and pretend to not want to sell it. If this happens, then walk away, you will usually be called back.

6) From then on, only lift your price by 5% at a time. You should be able to buy at half the price of the first price given.

斤 斤 计 较

jìn jìn jì jiào

to haggle over every ounce

Lunar New Year

The oldest and most important festival in China is the Spring Festival, more commonly known in the West as Lunar New Year or Chinese New Year.

恭
gōng

喜
xǐ

发
fā

财
cái

Congratulations and be prosperous

When is Chinese New Year?

Like other Chinese festivals, the new year is determined by the lunar calendar so the date of the holiday varies from late January to mid February.

It is on the day of the second new moon after the winter solstice.

Timetable of events

A few days before: Houses are thoroughly cleaned (to sweep away bad luck), debts repaid, hair cut and new clothes bought. Chinese people believe the new year must start cleanly, or it may continue in the way it begins... Doors are decorated with vertical scrolls of characters on red paper (like the ones on this page). Red is a lucky colour.

出
chū

入
rù

平
píng

安
ān

Peace and safety wherever you are

On New Year's Eve a reunion dinner is held where members of the family, near and far, get together to celebrate. The dinner is a sumptuous meal and dumplings (thought to resemble gold nuggets) are eaten. Most stay up till midnight, when firecrackers and fireworks are lit, to scare away evil spirits.

New Year's Day is spent visiting neighbours, family, and friends. Red packets containing 'lucky money' are given by married relatives to unmarried junior members of the household. A dragon or lion dance troupe may perform to drive out bad spirits.

The 15th Day is a public holiday. The New Year holiday lasts seven days in Mainland China, but the festival traditionally lasts till the 15th day of the lunar month and ends with the 'Lantern Festival'. Here, houses are decorated with colourful lanterns and people eat special food.

烟火
yānhuǒ
fireworks

新年快乐!
Xīnnián kuàilè!
Happy New Year!

Festival!

There are other major festivals in China.

Qing Ming

This is a day that Chinese people spend remembering and honouring their ancestors, and is sometimes called Tomb-Sweeping Day.

清 明

Qīng Míng

Paper gifts are burnt as offerings for the departed.

Mid-Autumn Festival

This festival happens during the full moon closest to the Autumn equinox. At this time the moon is at its fullest and brightest – the best time to celebrate the abundance of the summer's harvest. Everyone eats mooncakes and family and friends get together to admire the harvest moon, lighting up the barbecue. Children often carry around brightly coloured lanterns.

中 秋 节

Zhōng qiū jié

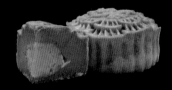

Mooncakes are often eaten in small slices with a cup of tea.

Dragon Boat Festival

This festival is celebrated yearly to commemorate the death of a famous Chinese poet, Qu Yuan, who drowned on the fifth day of the fifth lunar month more than 2000 years ago. The Dragon Boat Festival is celebrated by boat races in which the boats are decorated like dragons. Competing teams row their boats forward to a drumbeat, racing to reach the finish line.

端午节

Dūan wǔ jié

The standard crew has 10 pairs of rowers, one drummer, and one steerer.

Conversation practice 7

Test yourself on what you have learnt in this section.

Q. **Can you translate this conversation into Chinese?**

❶ What are you doing today?

❷ This morning I am going to Tiananmen Square.

❸ This afternoon, I am going to the market to buy some souvenirs.

A. **Here it is in Chinese.**

❶ 今天你想做什么?
Jīntiān nǐ xiǎng zuò shénme?

❷ 上午我去天安门
Shàngwǔ wǒ qù Tiān'ānmén
广场。
Guǎngchǎng.

❸ 下午我去市场买
Xiàwǔ wǒ qù shìchǎng mǎi
纪念品。
jìniànpǐn.

Q. **Can you translate these into Chinese?**

❶ How much is it?

❷ It's too expensive!

❸ Please say it again.

❹ I don't understand.

❺ Happy New Year!

A. **Here are the correct translations.**

❶ 多少钱?
Duōshǎo qián?

❷ 太贵了!
Tài guì le!

❸ 请你再说。
Qǐng nǐ zài shuō.

❹ 我听不懂。
Wǒ tīng bù dǒng.

❺ 新年快乐!
Xīnnián kuài lè!

Useful words

Use this list of words as quick reference and to improve your Chinese vocabulary.

aeroplane	fēijī	飞机
afternoon	xiàwǔ	下午
also	yě	也
apple	píngguǒ	苹果
arm	gēbo	胳膊
at	zài	在
autumn	qiūtiān	秋天
to be	shì	是
below	xià	下
bicycle	zìxíngchē	自行车
big	dà	大
bill	mǎidān	买单
bird	niǎo	鸟
birthday	shēngri	生日
book	shū	书
brother – older	gēge	哥哥
brother – younger	dìdi	弟弟
bus	gōnggòngqìchē	公共汽车

business	mǎimài	买卖
to buy	mǎi	买
to be called	jiào	叫
car	qìchē	汽车
China	Zhōngguó	中国
chopsticks	kuàizi	筷子
to climb	pá	爬
cold	lěng	冷
difficult	nán	难
to do	zuò	做
dog	gǒu	狗
to drink	hē	喝
ear	ěrduo	耳朵
east	dōng	东
easy	róngyì	容易
to eat	chī	吃
to enter	jìn	进
eye	yǎnjing	眼睛
father	bàba	爸爸
foot	jiǎo	脚
friend	péngyou	朋友
garden	huāyuán	花园

to give	gěi	给
to go	qù	去
good	hǎo	好
goodbye	zàijiàn	再见
grandfather	zǔfù	祖父
grandmother	zǔmǔ	祖母
hair	tóufa	头发
hand	shǒu	手
to have	yǒu	有
he	tā	他
head	tóu	头
hello	nǐ hǎo	你好
horse	mǎ	马
hot	rè	热
I	wǒ	我
left	zuǒbian	左边
leg	tuǐ	腿
to like	xǐhuan	喜欢
to love	ài	爱
man	nánrén	男人
Mandarin Chinese	pǔtōnghuà	普通话
map	dìtú	地图

market	shìchǎng	市场
menu	càidān	菜单
month	yuè	月
morning	shàngwǔ	上午
mother	māma	妈妈
mountain	shān	山
mouth	zuǐba	嘴巴
noodles	miàntiáo	面条
north	běi	北
nose	bízi	鼻子
Olympics	Àoyùnhuì	奥运会
on	shàng	上
panda	xióngmāo	熊猫
person	rén	人
to play (a sport)	dǎ	打
please	qǐng	请
restaurant	fàndiàn	饭店
rice	mǐfàn	米饭
right	yòubian	右边
to see	kàn	看
she	tā	她
sister – older	jiějie	姐姐

sister – younger	mèimei	妹妹
to sit	zuò	坐
small	xiǎo	小
snowy	xià xuě	下雪
sorry	duìbuqǐ	对不起
south	nán	南
souvenir	jìniànpǐn	纪念品
spring	chūntiān	春天
stomach	dùzi	肚子
to study	xuéxí	学习
summer	xiàtiān	夏天
taxi	chūzūqìchē	出租汽车
tea	chá	茶
teacher	lǎoshī	老师
teahouse	cháguǎn	茶馆
thank you	xièxie	谢谢
then	ránhòu	然后
this	zhè	这
ticket	piào	票
today	jīntiān	今天
toilet	cèsuǒ	厕所
tomorrow	míngtiān	明天

too	tài	太
traffic jam	dǔchē	堵车
train	huǒchē	火车
tree	shù	树
to understand	dǒng	懂
vehicle	chē	车
very	hěn	很
waiter/waitress	fúwùyuán	服务员
to want	xiǎng	想
water	shuǐ	水
we	wǒmen	我们
west	xī	西
what	shénme	什么
where	nǎr	哪儿
which	nǎ	哪
windy	guā fēng	刮风
winter	dōngtiān	冬天
woman	nǚrén	女人
word (spoken)	huà	话
year	nián	年
yesterday	zuótiān	昨天
you	nǐ	你

Index

Picture credits

The publisher would like to thank the following for their kind permission to reproduce their photographs:
(Key: a-above; b-below/bottom; c-centre; f-far; l-left; r-right; t-top)

Alamy Images: Beaconstox 118br; Cn Boon 59ca; Peter Bowater 73clb; Jon Bower 117tr; David Bowman 117cl; Wendy Connett 75crb, 80bl; Content Mine International 38cra; Dbimages/Betty Johnson 112-113; Dbimages/Derek Brown 73cl; Juergen Effner 82bl; Kevin Foy 73tl, 75br, 77t; Mike Goldwater 75tr; Tim Graham 75ftr; Henry Westheim Photography 104; Ids Photography 78tl; JLImages 102cr; Lou Linwei 103tr; Iain Masterton 82cl, 113cra; Neil McAllister 101cr; Panorama Media (Beijing) Ltd. 71bl; Panorama Media (Beijing) Ltd./Panorama Stock 101tl; Pictorial Press Ltd 38fcra; Giles Robberts 99tl; SAS 73cla, 83cla; Lynn Seldon 82cla; Bjorn Svensson 75fbr; Joe Tree 34ftr; View Stock 111clb. Corbis: 44-45, 109cr; Archivo Iconografico, S.A. 50crb; Diego Azubel/epa 101b; Dave Bartruff 90-91; Dean Conger 29bl; China Daily/Reuters 118cla; Tim Davis/DLILLC 73bl; Duomo 38cla; Kevin Foy 77tr; Jose Fuste Raga 109cl; Lowell Georgia 111tl; Lars Halbauer/dpa 77br, 102bl; Dallas and John Heaton/Free Agents Limited 109cra; Paul Hilton 71tr; So Hing-Keung 119cb; Wolfgang Kaehler 23br, 103cr; Jason Lee/Reuters 117b; Liu Liqun 71br, 100cb, 111bl, 114bl; Ken Liu 71tl; Yang Liu 75cra, 99cra; James Marshall 93bl; Mike McQueen 51br, 100c; Gideon Mendel 96-97, 114c; Michael Prince 49cra; Reuters 118bl; Peter Turnley 62bl; Nik Wheeler 111cla. Empics Ltd: Associated Press 103b. Flickr.com: cultureshock013 115bl; Kazuhiko Harada 83bl. Getty Images: Asia Images/Alex Mares-Manton 59br; Asia Images/Marcus Mok 19tr; The Bridgeman Art Library 17; Iconica/Antonio Mo 37tc, 37tl, 37tr; The Image Bank/LWA 63br; Lonely Planet Images/Phil Weymouth 92bl; National Geographic/Richard Nowitz 15clb; Stone/Jason Hosking 35tr. NASA: 14cla. PunchStock: Blend Images 29cl.

All other images © Dorling Kindersley

For further information see: www.dkimages.com

Acknowledgements

Dorling Kindersley would like to thank: Caroline Bingham, Iris Chan, Caroline Purslow, Suzanne Thompson, and Fleur Star for editorial support; Claire Bowers, Rose Horridge and Rob Nunn for picture research. Calvin Quek and Xiao Yao in Beijing for editorial assistance. A special thanks to Jeremy and Annabel Greenwood, Christeen Duffy, and Graeme, Charlie, and Max Duffy.